Office Feng Shui
in a week

GRAHAM GUNN

Office Feng Shui in a week

GRAHAM GUNN

Hodder & Stoughton

A MEMBER OF THE HODDER HEADLINE GROUP

Orders: please contact Bookpoint Ltd, 39 Milton Park, Abingdon, Oxon OX14 4TD.
Telephone: (44) 01235 400414, Fax: (44) 01235 400454. Lines are open from 9.00 -
6.00, Monday to Saturday, with a 24 hour message answering service.
Email address: orders@bookpoint.co.uk

British Library Cataloguing in Publication Data
A catalogue record for this title is available from The British Library

ISBN 0 340 73812 X

First published 1999
Impression number   10   9   8   7   6   5   4   3   2   1
Year   2004   2003   2002   2001   2000   1999

Typeset by Multiplex Techniques Ltd, St Mary Cray, Kent.
Printed in Great Britain for Hodder & Stoughton Educational, a division of
Hodder Headline Plc, 338 Euston Road, London NW1 3BH by Cox & Wyman Ltd,
Reading, Berkshire.

in *the Institute*
of Management

F O U N D A T I O N

The mission of the Institute of Management (IM) is to promote the art and science of management.

The Institute embraces all levels of management from student to chief executive and supports its own Foundation which provides a unique portfolio of services for all managers, enabling them to develop skills and achieve management excellence.

For information on the various levels and benefits of membership, please contact:

Department HS
Institute of Management
Cottingham Road
Corby
Northants NN17 1TT
Tel: 01536 204222
Fax: 01536 201651

This series is commissioned by the Institute of Management Foundation.

C O N T E N T S

Graham Gunn is a management and feng shui consultant offering a broad-scope analysis of, and holistic, practical solutions to, complex business issues in all kinds of government and commercial organisations. He is based in London, England with Integral Dynamics U.K., which has the remit of assisting organisations and projects in defining the overall optimum path to their mission objectives.

Although he has been a student of Oriental philosophies for 30 years, his professional background is in the management of high-technology, multinational projects in Europe and the USA. He became interested in linking feng shui with modern research into living and working environments when faced with the problems of reducing the psychological stresses on astronauts for Europe's first manned spacecraft. Thereafter, he applied these ideas to high-stress, project office environments, schools, land development sites, homes and a host of small and large businesses.

Graham Gunn is a frequent contributor to the media on feng shui matters, and is author of *Harmonise Your Home – a No-nonsense Guide to Feng Shui and How to Use It*. He has presented talks on feng shui to the Institute of Directors and the Academy of Chief Executives, and holds one- and two-day workshops on practical feng shui and feng shui in business in the UK and other parts of Europe.

The basic concepts and ideas behind what is now called 'feng shui' were developed thousands of years ago in India, Tibet and China. Essentially, they were guidelines for selecting and creating healthy and safe living and working environments in which people could thrive. These concepts, however, went beyond the merely mechanical aspects of security and practicality which characterise the health and safety regulations of today. They also included more subtle psychological factors that affect the human subconscious, and their subsequent effects on our vitality, awareness, energy and drive. In addition, all of these elements were held in a framework of Taoist ethics and philosophy that simultaneously linked them to an awareness of the universal soul or spirit while grounding them to the natural environment of which our physical bodies and institutions are an integral part.

Although the fundamentals are very ancient, the term 'feng shui', in Oriental time scales, is quite modern, the earliest surviving reference being in the eleventh century. It appears, however, that in recent centuries, the subject became bound up in very complex and mysterious symbolism, rituals and dogma that made it somewhat inaccessible to many Westerners. The recent popularity of feng shui in the West has triggered a more analytical interpretation of the concepts, and we now find that these match very well with modern theology, psychology, anthropology, biology and environmental design principles.

Today, many organisations, from large multinational corporations to small shops, will hire the services of a feng shui consultant to advise on optimising the workplace environment, corporate identity and even strategic planning. This book focusses on some basic, yet profound feng shui methods for enhancing your office environment so that it supports you rather than sabotages you. The ultimate objective is to help you achieve more at work with less effort.

The seven-day breakdown of how best to employ basic feng shui in your office or workplace is structured as follows:

Sunday	Seeing with new eyes
Monday	Knowing what you really want
Tuesday	Clearing obstructions and blockages
Wednesday	Creating a more supportive environment
Thursday	Harmonising your workspace with your goals
Friday	Getting 'the best bang for the buck'
Saturday	Keeping your workspace working for you

Throughout the text, I have used the symbol (*) to indicate that further information on particular topics is available — see Guide to Resources at the end of Saturday's chapter.

I would like to acknowledge the great assistance given in the compilation of this work by my partner, Anna Rybaczynska.

Seeing with new eyes

There is a very strong connection between how we think, feel and act and the environments in which we live and work. It is important, therefore, to be aware of what these connections are so that you can start to use your workspace as an additional tool for creating the work experiences and career path that you want.

The first job in using feng shui is to become very conscious of the characteristics of your surroundings, and by working through the check list below, you will see your workplace as though for the first time. I suggest that you write out the answers to the questions that follow. It takes a bit longer but it really brings home the truth of the situation.

Q1 How or what do you usually feel when entering your workplace?

To answer this, think about what emotions you have as you approach the building, enter the building and move to your particular office or work station.

Notice if your breathing rate or pulse rate changes, or if there is a sense of anxiety, excitement, frustration or depression. Notice also if you have a sense of being overwhelmed or if any of your muscles start to become tense or if your posture changes. All these details are clues that can help you determine what aspects of your work environment might need to be changed.

Q2 What is the general appearance of your workplace?

Evaluate factors such as tidiness, cleanliness, whether the furniture is in good condition or not and if the paint work is damaged or marked. Are the windows clean? Notice how books, papers, files and so on are stored – in piles on your desk, the floor and shelves, and on top of cupboards and windowsills, or are things put away neatly in filing cabinets, drawers or bookcases? Does your office have dirty coffee cups, old newspapers and broken furniture lurking in half-forgotten corners or behind the filing cabinets?

Q3 What is the lighting like?

The amount, quality and distribution of light in your work area has a significant influence on how well and for how long you can function effectively. First, be aware of what natural daylight comes into your workspace at different times of the day and different seasons of the year. Also note what effect this has on your approach to work. For example, if you get very little or no natural daylight through most of the working day, check if extreme lethargy or mild depression build up as the week progresses and whether this is different from other places you have worked in where there may have been more natural light. Alternatively, you may get so much sunlight that the office overheats, reading becomes difficult because of glare, or the computer screen becomes impossible to see. Natural light is complemented by artificial lighting, but this too must be suitable for the work you are doing. Is there enough general lighting to keep your energy levels up, or is there too much for comfort? Do you have a desk lamp or other task-focussed lighting, and how much control do you have over the amount of light in your workspace? Look also for strong contrasts of light and shade in your field of view (for example, between the ceiling surface and the light fixtures), and note how colours are affected by the kind of lighting in the office.

Q4   How easy is it to move around?

How easy is it to get to your desk and settle down to work?
Are there wide, bright and clear corridors leading to your
office, or do you have to pass through a maze of narrow
passages or round banks of file cabinets and/or piles of
goods and products? Is your desk easy to get to, or do you
need to be something of a contortionist to squeeze between
other desks, lever yourself over the stack of unfiled
documents by the side of it or twist your body into the
chair? Once you are settled in, what is it like to get out
from your desk to meetings, the toilet or the drinks
machine, or to visit your stress-management consultant?

Q5   What is the colour scheme like?

The colours in your workspace can have a surprising
amount of influence on your personal energy levels,
concentration and creativity. Take note, therefore, of:

- the dominant colours (usually on the walls and floor)
- other significant colours (on furniture, doors, materials
  and equipment)
- the intensity, brightness or dullness of the colours
- colour contrasts – i.e. different adjacent colours or
  relative intensities.

Also notice your reactions to the colours around you. Do
they make you feel calm or tense, and are they pleasing to
look at or depressing? Although you may not have total
control over the general colour scheme of your office or
workplace, it is still useful to know how it is affecting you,
because in feng shui we can make some corrections or

counterbalances in areas that you can control, even if it is just your individual desk area.

Q6 What about seating and position?

Most people in offices sit down to work despite the current fashion in stand-up computer tables. But you can waste a great deal of personal energy in sitting if the design and arrangements of your desk and chair are not compatible with the physical actions involved in the work. There are of course health and safety standards governing the appropriate height of desks and adjustability of chairs, and there are many recommendations for optimum heights, angles and positions of computer screens (*). I suggest that you make your own assessment of how you sit at work using the following guidelines:

- Do you repeatedly get aches and pains in arms, wrists, shoulders, neck, torso, stomach, hips or legs while at work?
- Are the desk and chair heights correct for your physique?
- How do you normally hold your spine, head and shoulders – bent over or in a straight line?
- Do you have to sit for long periods with your torso slightly twisted in order to use a computer, telephone or other equipment?
- Does your chair give good support for your thighs, lumbar region, shoulders and head?
- Does your chair have armrests, and if so, are they adjustable?

Also note, when in your normal work position, what you are facing (e.g. computer screens, walls, other desks) and how close you are to them. Then observe what is directly behind your chair – door, window, wall, corridor, pictures, colleagues, electronic equipment etc.

Q7　What kind of ambient noise is there?

Noise can drain your energy in a very subtle, almost imperceptible way. It is therefore important to note what types and levels of noise you are being exposed to, even if you cannot change the situation immediately. Here are some typical sources of energy-draining sounds:

- telephones and fax machines
- other people's conversations
- road traffic, trains and aeroplanes
- computers, printers, scanners etc.
- air-conditioning systems
- drinks-dispensing machines
- buzzing fluorescent light tubes
- creaking chairs and doors

Q8   What aromas and smells are there?

Aromas and smells have effects at both the physical and psychological levels. Physically, they can indicate the presence of toxic chemicals in the air that can affect your performance. Psychologically, they can be associated with distracting thoughts, both pleasant and unpleasant. So notice what you smell when you enter your office space, such as:

- cigarette, pipe or cigar smoke
- fresh flowers or trees
- traffic fumes
- VOCs (volatile organic compounds emitted from printers, flooring, paints, computers, adhesives and solvents)
- perfumes
- artificial fragrances from cleaning materials
- coffee

Q9   What images and symbols are around you?

Your brain puts many interpretations on what you see. Some of these you are conscious of, but many lie very deep in your subconscious mind. This latter part of us has evolved over millions of years to respond automatically to anything that could be a survival threat. This was very useful to our ancestors who lived in the wild, but it can create a lot of unnecessary tension in the office of today. The other problem is that these reactions are 'hard wired' and don't get switched off until you die, so we need to know what they are and eliminate the stimulants as much as possible from our environment. Examine carefully, therefore, the following features of your workplace:

- pictures (people, places, things, abstracts)
- models and statues (products, corporate founders, icons)

- noticeboards and their contents
- whether office doors are normally open or closed
- patterns on walls and flooring
- whether your workplace contains lots of sharp corners, points or edges in furniture, structural features, plants or other decorative items
- the company logo and marketing materials

Summary

This is enough work for the first day. The important point is that you have really become more aware of what is around you each day, so that you can develop an understanding of how the environment can affect you and how you can modify it to get more of what you want. Determining clearly what you want, however, is Monday's task.

Knowing what you really want

Being clear about what you want to achieve with the help of your working environment and the changes instigated from the ideas presented in this book, is very important. Your mind can generate all kinds of solutions and pathways to your goals, but it needs help in focussing on a very few things at a time (between five and nine seems to be the currently accepted figure), otherwise it can become overloaded, confused, forgetful and careless. You can use feng shui principles to support it in this way.

The greatest philosophers say that you have all the tools and information you need right now to achieve your dreams. In fact, they say that you cannot even conceive an idea until, at some level, your body/mind/spirit system knows what to do with it. I hope that this encourages you to be free and uninhibited when defining what you want, but always remember that lasting success depends on the integrity of your desires. That means they should be aimed at the overall well-being of yourself and others and do not create division or separation or conflict between people.

EVERYTHING YOU NEED...

Before attempting to define our goals and objectives, it is worth taking a fresh look at your 'wants and needs' environment. The best way to do this is to create a 'map' like the one shown in the diagram, to help clarify and structure your current experience and perceptions.

What I want and have ⊞	What I want and don't have ⊟
• interesting job • good co-workers • modern equipment	• better communication skills • new ideas for marketing X • area manager position
What I don't want and have ⊟	What I don't want and don't have ⊞
• eye strain and tiredness • too much noise in the office • uneasy relationship with boss	• responsibility for sales • work in a large office • a cold office

'Wants and needs' map

This model of your experience drives you to recognise those elements of your working life that are present, as well as those that may be missing. With this information, it is possible to see a more complete and accurate picture of what the real issues are and so to be more selective about the most important 'wants'. This concept of goal determination comes from the area of *neuro-linguistic programming*.

Feng shui offers an additional useful perspective on our desires and goals. This is based on the ideas of harmony and balance that underpin Taoist philosophy. The simplest way to describe this is by using the diagram shown.

④ Prosperity	⑨ Recognition, acknowledgement	② Relationship, marriage
③ Parents, teachers	⑤ Physical and mental health	⑦ Creativity, children
⑧ Self-awareness	① Path, career	⑥ Helpers, friends, experience

The nine primary aspects of life

This model states that for good overall physical and mental health, the primary aspects of life defined in the surrounding segments must be in balance. To explain what I mean by this, here are some examples.

If you want to improve the quality of the principal relationships in your life, it is advisable to work also on the complementary aspect of self-awareness: who you are, why you exist, what is beyond body and mind etc. It is hard to have a sound relationship with others until you get to grips with yourself. There is an enormous number of books, tapes, seminars and groups available these days to support you in this way.

If one of your goals requires greater creativity or imagination on your part, you may need also to look in your past experience for unresolved issues that occupy your subconscious mind and obstruct the free flow of ideas and insights. Quite often, we are inhibited by painful memories or negative comments from parents, teachers or work colleagues and it is necessary to resolve these within you and let them go. You would be amazed at how much of your life is still influenced by seemingly trivial and irrelevant events from many years ago. Again, there are many possibilities for clearing this kind of mental clutter.

It is also useful to use this model to understand what you do well. For example, if you have become more prosperous (in the broadest sense), the chances are that you have helped many people and gained a great deal of experience along the way, since the 'Helpers, friends, experience' aspect is the complementary opposite of the 'Prosperity' aspect. To continue to be prosperous, you now know the kinds of key strategies and behaviours that you need to maintain.

You can see that in this model, if your goal falls into one particular aspect of life, you will also need to work on its complementary, opposite aspect. There can be additional secondary benefits from examining the situation in the two supporting aspects of the complementary opposite, as shown in the diagram.

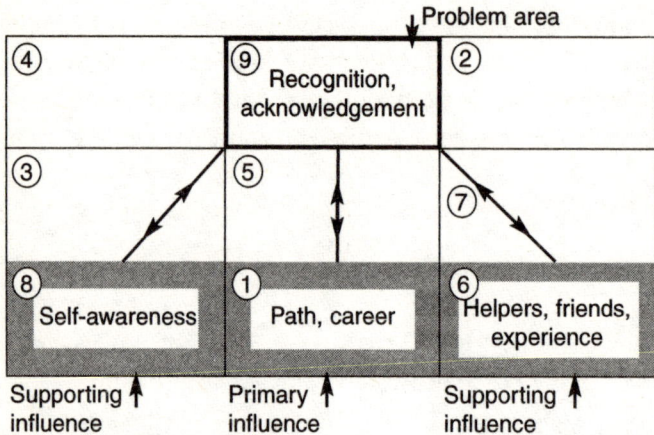

Triangular aspect relationships

We can translate the nine aspects of life in this model into equivalent aspects for the typical office environment as follows:

① Path/career — The opportunities and potential outcomes of the job you currently hold.

② Relationship, marriage — The quality of your interaction with your closest work colleagues or partners.

③ Parents, teachers — Your own beliefs and attitudes, or those of a strong boss or the corporate culture.

④ Prosperity — The quality and standards of the people in the company, its equipment and premises.

⑤ Health — Your physical, mental and emotional well-being in the work environment.

⑥ Helpers, friends, experience — The experiences you have through interactions with all the people in your work environment.

⑦ Creativity, children	Your creative ideas, pet projects and adaptability to new situations.
⑧ Self-awareness	Understanding of your job, role in the company or personal attributes and behaviours.
⑨ Recognition	Acknowledgement in the form of awards, pay rises, promotions, 'thank you' notes, friendships.

So, figuring out and optimising your goals and objectives can be quite an involved process. It is worthwhile to do this properly, however, since you will use the results on Thursday to select specific changes to your office space.

To help create a more holistic array of 'wants', I suggest that you consider three main areas:

1) the development of your inner resources, skills, experience;
2) the quantity and quality of the work that you do;
3) your career or business goals.

1   Inner resources

You never stop learning, whether you like this idea or not. Generally, life gets easier if you plan and structure your learning to suit the visions that you have, rather than hope that you will spontaneously have the required knowledge and skills at your fingertips when the need is right in front of you. So consider therefore what would be really handy for you to know about that can perhaps save you time and money, open up new opportunities or generally make life more enjoyable.

There are of course all the practical skills that you could develop: using new computer software, typing, management techniques, negotiation and language skills, feng shui and so on. There are also skills that can have a more indirect, but often more substantial impact on your life, such as healthy eating, self-awareness (e.g. through meditation, eneagrams, astrology, philosophy), music, art and physical exercise (including t'ai chi or yoga). All of these (and many others besides) can help you to get to know more about yourself and to take more control over the direction your life takes.

2   Quantity and quality of work

You may also have other 'wants' with regard to the type of work that you do or the way in which you do it. There is a wide range of possibilities here, including:

- working faster
- being more creative
- reducing the amount of effort and stress required
- being more assertive/effective/authoritative
- thinking and/or expressing yourself more clearly
- making better plans or forecasts
- making things run more smoothly

These are quite abstract as written here, and you need to add some specifics to them otherwise your mind cannot respond effectively. For example, working faster may mean, to you, processing an average of 20 sales orders per hour rather than 10, or generating six contract proposals per month instead of four.

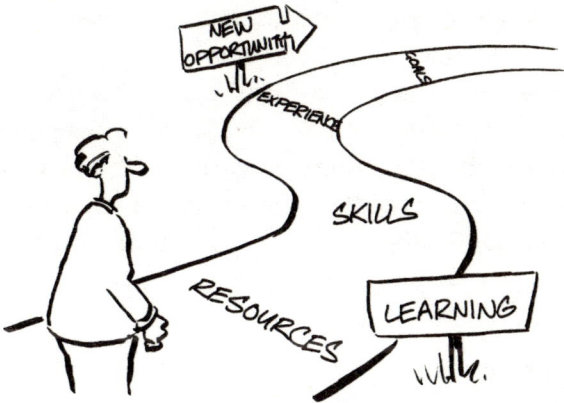

Being more creative can be quantified in terms of finding three new product outlets next month, or generating an innovative, exciting way of marketing your own (or your client's) accountancy services, or selling the excessive number of second-hand cars on your forecourt.

To specify stress reductions, you must first be clear about what the main stresses are. For example, you may find that your back aches halfway through the day, in which case your 'want' is to remain painless all day, every day. Maybe telephone interruptions are draining your concentration and energy, so make it your goal to have two consecutive hours per day of complete isolation by the end of the month.

Assertiveness, effectiveness and authoritativeness are all associated with the quality of your communications. Set out your goal in the form, for example, of finding out why you frequently fail to be understood by so-and-so, and then correcting this situation; or of increasing the percentage of requests that you make which are properly carried out to 90 per cent by July.

Making things run more smoothly could simply involve deciding to eliminate at least one time-wasting or duplicated process each month in your area of work or responsibility. In my experience, a common disruption to efficient operations is in the storage and retrieval of the information people need to conduct their work effectively. A goal to smooth out this aspect of a business can have wondrous economic effects.

3   Goals

Defining your career or business 'wants' may appear more straightforward: a 30 per cent sales increase by March, a regional-manager position by November, etc. There may also be subtler, but nonetheless genuine 'wants' such as receiving acknowledgement for the work that you do. This can be expressed through pay, promotion, verbal appreciation, presents, respect and so on. If it is your own business, perhaps it is its public image that you want to change in certain specific ways: reliability, quality product or services, friendly atmosphere, modern and efficient, etc.

Another aspect to consider is any unfulfilled desire you may have to influence the events in your work, or the path the business takes, or the freedom you have for taking initiative and responsibility and having the corresponding authority. Quite often, very capable people who could generate many benefits for their company feel constrained or inhibited by their apparent status or their own lack of self-confidence. If you can relate to this and are no longer willing to accept the frustration, make it your goal to be heard and acknowledged.

Hopefully, your mind is now buzzing with all kinds of
desires and goals, so it is beneficial to write them all down
in the categories described above. You will probably have
far too many to handle all at once, so you need to sub-
divide them into time frames: short-term (within a few
weeks, say), medium-term (within a few months or a
couple of years) and long-term (more than five years). After
this process, it may be necessary to prioritise them further:
class A = essential; class B = very useful; class C = nice to
have if at all possible. This should give you a basis for
selecting the few most important things you want your
workplace to support you in achieving right now.

Summary

Today, we have looked at how to map and plan for your wants, needs and goals at the workplace. Tomorrow, we will get started on clearing the way to making these come to fruition.

Clearing obstructions and blockages

Probably the most important concept in feng shui is the idea of harmony and balance, as represented by the yin/yang symbol.

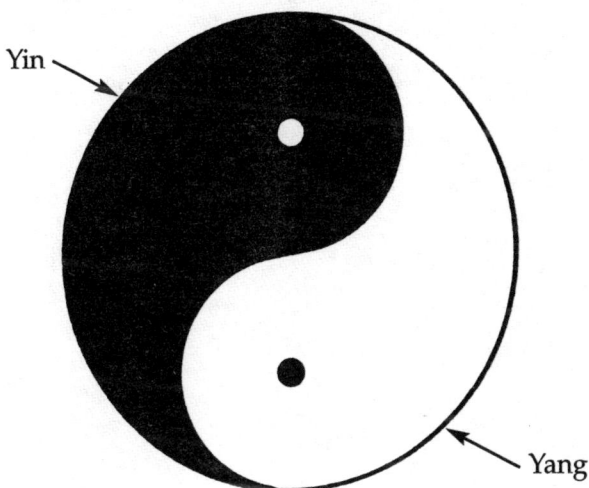

Yin

Yang

The yin/yang symbol

Yin and yang represent the relative qualities of different aspects of energy. For example, when considering energy in the form of light, bright light is considered to be yang while darkness is yin. Twilight is more yang than darkness but more yin than full daylight. Below is a list of the relative yin and yang qualities for other aspects of energy:

Yin	Yang
cold	hot
still/calm	moving/active
relaxing	energising
descending	rising
curved shapes	angular shapes
quiet	noisy
plain and simple	complex and cluttered
soft	hard
light	heavy
weak	strong
dark	bright
no contrast	high contrast

violet   indigo   blue   green   yellow   orange   red

The idea in feng shui is to use this model to maintain a balance both within your physical environment and between that environment and yourself. For example, if your office does not have many windows or receives little direct sunlight and you persistently feel tired (i.e. it is very yin in this respect), then you would compensate for this by adding more yang characteristics such as artificial lighting or objects that move. This creates a more energising environment. Also, if your work seems very complex and

hectic and you find it hard to manage things calmly and
without stress (i.e. your working lifestyle may be too yang),
then it is advisable to create a more yin environment with
softer lighting, curved or round images or objects, a simple
decor and quiet colours.

If you have the opportunity to design an office from
scratch, the best approach for creating harmony using
yin/yang principles is to make the basic features relatively
yin, focussing initially on noise control, optimum lighting
and the colour scheme (see Wednesday's activities), and
then add yang elements such as bright pictures, plants,
coloured lamps and so on until you feel that the correct
balance has been reached. In this way, it is easier to
energise or calm a space by simply adding or removing
things.

Bear in mind also that rooms allocated to tasks which
require detailed work and high concentration should be
more yin in style than rooms used for meetings or

brainstorming sessions. One other point is that going to the extremes of either yin or yang conditions leads to the exact opposite. For example, if your lifestyle is hectic, your office noisy, cluttered and painted everywhere in strong, bright colours, you live a very yang life. Chances are that you will soon become exhausted and very ill – which is an extreme yin condition. Moderation in all things is the message and the yin/yang theory helps you to find this.

We shall be using yin and yang extensively on Wednesday in reducing typical vitality-draining characteristics of the modern office environment, but it is also very useful in explaining the effects of physical blockages and obstructions in the office. Obstructions to getting our work done or our ideas manifested come in a wide variety of guises. Some are obvious and direct while others are more subtle and indirect. If you have completed Sunday's tasks properly, you have probably already identified many of the more obvious physical obstructions to your work. You can categorise these in terms of:

- obstructions to getting into the office or building. These might include a very dark and/or narrow doorway, corridor, stairs or elevator, a security barrier or piles of incoming or outgoing products. While you physically overcome such barriers every day, and perhaps take little notice of them, your subconscious mind sees only 'obstruction' and the whole of your work experience can gradually become linked to the idea of struggle and difficulty. You can imagine what this does to your enthusiasm and energy over time! If you do not own the company, you probably don't have much control over the design of the entrance, but at least you are aware of the issue and thus are less stressed by it, and you can always make suggestions to the boss or recommend a good feng shui consultant to help identify suitable remedies!

- obstructions to getting to your desk or workplace. After entering your office building, do you walk freely and easily to your desk or work station, quickly get comfortable and settle down to the business of the day, or is the journey from the office door to your desk more reminiscent of a marine commando assault training course? If getting to your desk involves negotiating a path round a maze of filing cabinets, other desks, partitions and piles of books or files on the floor, then a significant part of your daily energy is used up in this way. Again, you may not have much control over this situation, but you might look at what is immediately surrounding your own desk and find ways to clear it.
- obstructions at your desk or work station. You need room to manoeuvre your arms and legs, to easily access drawers, the computer, the waste bin and so on. There needs to be enough space behind your chair for getting to and from your desk easily and for the occasional leaning back to physically, as well as mentally, take a broader perspective on your work. So, do whatever you can to clear the space under, on top of, or around your desk to give you freedom of movement.

These kinds of obstructions can be defined as very yin characteristics. To bypass them takes more physical effort, which is yang. As the yin condition gets worse, people waste more and more time and energy, and the business stagnates. Another form of obstruction, but this time the

opposite way round in yin/yang terms, is represented by chaos and clutter in the office. When a workplace is a total mess, your concentration and energy are scattered – a very yang condition. The result is that very little effective work gets done, and the business declines – a very yin condition.

You see, the universe is always in balance and harmony, but it may not be your own preferred state of balance and harmony. Here are some typical examples of office clutter, with potential solutions.

1   General office untidiness.

Notice how different you feel when walking into a clean, spacious and neat office, compared with a cluttered, untidy office. If you are faced with a mess when you get to work, find a few minutes each day to sort it out. It is often more practical in busy offices to do this gradually, but persistence, determination and cooperation from colleagues is the key to success here. Easy things to do might include disposing of dirty cups, out-of-date catalogues, newspapers and magazines, and dead or dried-up plants. You might also purge the office noticeboard of the chaotic array of faded photos, layers of irrelevant messages, invitations to the Christmas party of 10 years ago, and so on.

Less frequent are opportunities for the revolutionary approach where the whole office is cleared, restructured and transformed in one big purge. Success here depends on well-defined objectives and requirements, a good project plan and an even better project manager.

2   Cluttered desk space

If your desk is covered with books, papers, floppy disks and files, this also represents an obstruction to clear thinking and getting work completed quickly. You will spend a lot of time searching for things, whether it's the urgent 'phone messages from yesterday or the report you must review by this afternoon, or a paper clip. Yes, I know,

you are expected to handle 20 different tasks at once, and there is nowhere else to keep the reference materials that you need. So what can be done? Here are some suggestions for reducing desk clutter:

- Some of the paperwork is out of date or long past its 'use by' date. Throw these papers away.
- Use a 'day book' or a large page-per-day diary or a good-sized personal organiser to jot down the messages, meeting invitations, customer data etc. This can help remove many odd pieces of paper and information from the desk.
- If you use a computer with useful administration software (e.g. with a diary, e-mail package, names/addresses database), use this to store information that would otherwise lie around on scraps of paper.
- For easy access to new or important data related to your current projects or tasks, try one of those desktop multi-drawer storage boxes. This will help keep things in order and reduce some of the clutter. (Tip: don't keep the box on your desktop!)

There is a very comprehensive book on this subject called *Clear Your Desk*, which is written by Declan Treacy(*).

3   The filing system

Despite the idea that computers would lead to a 'paperless' office, the reality is that there is just as much paper floating around (if not more) than before. While it is important for everyone to consciously eliminate unnecessary paper, office managers or administrators often do not provide enough storage facilities for the paper that remains, and this leads to the clutter and chaos seen in many offices. In addition, because there is a lack of organised filing, individuals are tempted to hoard documents for fear of not having access to critical information later. This contributes to yet more clutter and chaos. *Clear Your Desk* has a number of suggestions in this regard which you may find applicable to your situation. For large or complex multidimensional projects, however, more elaborate systems are often needed.

I developed a 'File Codes Indexing System' for some very large space programs. All types of information – status reports, test data, contracts, product catalogues, specifications, drawings, schedules, invoices – were coded in a consistent logical way regardless of the storage medium (i.e. paper, microfiche, computer disc). Everything was retained in a central data bank and engineers and managers of all kinds quickly learned where to find the information needed. The result: 3 or 4 copies of key documents were required instead of 30 or 40, and individual offices and workstations were liberated from tons of surplus reports and reference material(*).

Summary

Having now removed much of the clutter from your office, you can begin to see more clearly what other types of energy-sapping features there may be around you. But let's leave this until tomorrow.

Creating a more supportive environment

You may have heard that feng shui is about'energy' in a building. You may also have considered that it is not a particularly informative description. In practical terms, what we are in fact dealing with is how the design of the environment affects the vitality of the people (or the living organisms) in it.

Environment designs can be exciting, awe inspiring, comforting, relaxing, dull, irritating or downright unpleasant in any number of ways. In other words an office space can stimulate your vitality and creativity or drain them.

Before thinking about what is needed to create a stimulating environment, however, we should consider reducing those attributes that drain your vitality. The most common ones (other than the blockages dealt with on Tuesday) are described below.

1   Noise

From many surveys and studies carried out in Europe and the USA, noise, especially sudden, harsh noise, is considered to be the most disruptive factor in offices – noise from computers, printers, copy machines, traffic, telephones, air-conditioning systems, conversations, and so on. Unfortunately, noise is one of the most difficult factors for you to deal with alone, especially if you work in a large open-plan office. However, here are some suggestions that are worth trying:

- Place some vibration-absorbing material under your computer or under any other vibrating equipment on your desk. Cork tiles can work well in this way and have the additional benefit of containing some of the electromagnetic fields generated by such equipment.

- Minimise orange and especially yellow colours in your workspace. These colours are known to stimulate loud talking and noise. Introduce soft greens or blues, which tend to calm and quieten the atmosphere.
- If there is none already, put some carpeting material around your desk to absorb the sound of people walking close to your workspace.
- Oil any squeaky chairs, doors or other equipment in your working vicinity.

If you and your colleagues feel that you would be more productive in a quieter environment, it may be worth approaching company management with a request for action. Possibilities include sound-absorbing partitions, removing drinks-dispenser machines, printers, photocopiers etc. from the general working area, installing sound-absorbing carpeting, removing computers from desktops to carriers below, installing triple glazing (to reduce noise from traffic or other external sources) and creating dedicated enclosed areas for meetings and discussions.

2   Light and lighting

The second most energy-draining factors in offices,
according to formal studies, is inadequate or inappropriate
lighting. Lighting engineers are obliged to meet specified
levels of 'illuminance' which is defined as the amount of
light impinging on a flat horizontal surface. The human eye
however, actually experiences another factor, confusingly
referred to as 'luminance'. This is a function of the colours
and textures in the environment, the distribution of light from
ceiling, walls and other surfaces, the spectrum of the light
source itself and the overall size and complexity of the space.

Ideally, the background lighting in an office should be
reasonably bright but not excessively bright. It should have
minimal harsh light/shade contrasts yet contain some
variation in intensity to help some people orient themselves
easier and judge space and distance. The light should also
be as close as possible to normal daylight in terms of its
spectral quality and polarization. The lighting on specific
work areas (task lighting) should be a little more intense than
the background level. Unfortunately, most office lighting is
uniformly harsh and uncomfortable, with colour-distorting
flourescent luminaires set into 'egg-crate' ceiling panels.

If you work in such an office, you may not have much
control over the general lighting quality or lighting level,
but you may be able to adjust the light environment around
your own desk space. Here are some suggestions.

What if you feel that the general light level is too strong?

- Try wearing polarised sunglasses.
- If the lighting is from ordinary fluorescent tubes which
  have a spectrum output which peaks in the yellow region

of the visible spectrum, and is biased towards the blue end, place more red items around you, since red absorbs blue light.

- If the lighting is from 'daylight' tubes, keep darker-coloured items around you so that less light is reflected into your eyes. You could use dark-coloured versions of mouse mats, desk pads, diaries and notebooks, pocket files etc.

- If your work surface is white or a very light colour, use a large darker-coloured desk pad, but preferably not black as this would create a harsh, uncomfortable contrast with white papers.

- If you cannot read the computer screen due to glare from windows or artificial lights, fit a polarising filter over the screen or make a shade (cardboard works quite well) extending from the top and sides of the monitor.

- You may be able to remove some of the lamps from the luminaires in the ceiling to reduce the general light level.

What if you feel that the general light level is too dull?

- Buy a desk lamp that focusses light on your work area. Avoid those with ordinary fluorescent tubes since these are noisy and distort colours. There are tubes that have a spectrum that is closer to natural daylight and that also carry polarising filters (*). Alternatively, use incandescent or halogen lamps, but ensure that these are properly shaded so that the light source itself is not in your direct view, otherwise you will suffer eyestrain.

- Even though you may spend much time looking down at your desk, research shows that you are more often looking within 20 degrees (up or down) from the

horizontal. Therefore, if your environment seems dull, you could direct additional desk lamps to shine on the walls around you.
- Lighten the walls or other surfaces around you with paint, pictures or posters.
- Have lighter-coloured objects on your desk.
- If your desk surface is black, use a large light-coloured desk pad to cover it.

There is a wide range of modern lighting and control systems now available that offer many possibilities for making the office environment appear more natural and less stressful. There are luminaires producing light with a spectrum and polarization that is very close to natural daylight. There are also dimmer systems that automatically adjust the output of luminaires in different parts of an office, to compensate for changes in sunlight levels. In addition, the latest switching systems allow for great flexibility and personal control of the local illumination level, by using remote control switches. These can be placed at any convenient location around, or on, or even under your desk. They are not connected to electrical cables (thus very quick and easy to install or move) and can be programmed to control any of the existing ceiling or wall mounted luminaires (*). This is one of the most useful ideas I have seen recently, and is applicable to any enclosed environment.

3   Temperature and humidity

There are regulations on all kinds of environmental factors in the workplace, including temperature and humidity levels. These are designed to meet the needs of the 'average' person, but we all know that offices are full of individuals with individual requirements that change from time to time. In fact, the third most disturbing factor noted in office environment studies concerns the atmospheric temperature and humidity. Yet again, in most large offices the individual may have little control over these factors, but here are some 'self help' suggestions anyway.

If you feel too cold:

- wear more clothes (sorry if this sounds too obvious!)
- add red or orange elements to your office decor
- add more lights
- stick a plastic or cardboard cover over the vent of an overenthusiastic office air-conditioning system.

If you feel too hot:

- use more cool blue or green colours around the office, either by painting the walls, adding plants, changing the pictures or posters or selecting different-coloured items on your desk.
- add water to your environment in a glass or bowl on your desk or on surrounding surfaces. You may even take a miniature water fountain to the office to symbolise freshness and coolness.
- put pictures of icy seas or mountains on the walls.
- keep yourself feeling fresh with antiperspirants or deodorants, but beware: use only those brands which do not contain toxic chemicals such as propylene glycol (which gets absorbed through the skin and into the blood and then is stored in your liver potentially causing

problems with eyes, hair and immune system) or aluminium compounds that have been linked to Alzheimer's disease(*).

If you feel too dry:

- put a ceramic or hard plastic container of water over any radiators or other heaters that are turned on.
- put porous earthenware pots of water around the office. (Some unglazed ceramic wine coolers can be used for this purpose.)
- add more lush plants to ionise and release moisture into the air.
- drink lots of water (at least 2 litres per day). Preferably, stand the water on an 'energising' device that breaks up clumps of water and mineral molecules, thus making them both more bio-available (*).
- keep your skin moist by using creams or sprays that are based on natural products and humectants. (Humectants are large molecules that our bodies produce in abundance when we are young. They attract and hold water vapour on the surface of the skin, thus keeping it moist and cool.) Do not use so-called 'moisturising' products that contain mineral oils or glycols: these are lubricants, not moisturisers, and will make you feel even worse (*)!

If you are distracted by thermal discomfort at work, It is hard to concentrate on what you are supposed to be doing, and this leads to stress and loss of your vital energy. In the United States, some companies have developed thermal and air conditioning systems for each individual workstation. While this might be going a bit too far for

most businesses, it does indicate how much employee
comfort is (and should be) recognised as a key performance
factor.

4   Seating

I remember when PCs first appeared in the office
environment; they were promoted as a great new extension
to the human brain. But we now seem to have created a
situation where the human body has been relegated to an
extension of the PC. The primary posture during working
hours for millions of people is conditioned by the demands
of the computer, and this unnatural situation can be a great
source of muscular strain and tension. It is time to redress
the balance.

Good office seating should provide solid body support in a
variety of postures over the required periods of time. There
should be no or very little muscular effort involved in
sitting, and blood circulation in the thighs and legs should
be unobstructed (*).

The ideal office chair has the following basic characteristics:

- height adjustment to suit your physical characteristics
- armrests to give support and increase your sense of
  security
- multiple adjustments (to the angle of the seat, back and
  armrests) to meet different postural requirements
- a high backrest that supports the pelvic and lumbar
  regions, middle back and shoulders
- a firm but well-padded seat with a moisture-permeable
  fabric cover

- a strong construction with no looseness or wobbles in the adjustment mechanisms (a wobbly seat can indicate or, indeed, create an unstable or insecure job or business situation)
- a five-arm star base with firmly fitted castors or glides

If the chair you are supplied with is not to this standard, ask to get it replaced or buy your own chair – after all, it is your body that is affected. Alternatively, use cushions or foot rests to compensate temporarily for an inadequate chair.

5   Images and symbols

Even the pictures on the walls of your office can drain your energy and make work seem harder than it is. You may not be aware of it, but modern research suggests that our brains constantly evaluate and process everything our senses pick up – consciously or otherwise. For example, when your eyes see abstract or obscure images, the mind feels obliged to figure out what is there and whether it is safe or a threat. This processing uses up a tiny part of your energy and happens automatically, and when this happens many times each day, the cumulative effect over months and years can have a considerable impact on your success and enjoyment of life.

Other images that can create unnecessary stress or inappropriate behaviour patterns include:

- scenes of desolation, isolation or abandonment
- drab, dull colours or excessive black and white pictures
- scenes of destruction, sinking ships, battles etc.
- large areas of harsh, contrasting colours
- images with lots of sharp angles, points and edges
- images of storms, hurricanes, blizzards
- images of swords, daggers, missiles, guns
- images of sunsets, waterfalls, anything going down
- an excessive number of images from the past
- images of people who had sad endings (e.g. Marilyn Monroe)
- images of anything dead – plants, fish, animals, people

Positive images for the office (*) include those of:

- sunrises, birds or aeroplanes taking off, anything going up
- bright rural scenes, beaches, mountains and lakes
- bright flowers, trees, anything growing
- people working or playing together
- natural movement – birds flying, sailing boats, fish swimming
- happy, successful people, great teachers or leaders
- gently flowing water or clear pathways
- elegant, prosperous-looking cityscapes, parks and gardens

Also remember that we are making our environment more representative of that in which our species evolved. This allows the 'primitive' part of our brain to feel more at home, and thus cause fewer problems and distractions for the 'thinking' part of our brain. Plenty of healthy plants and at least some representation of water (or even a fish tank), will have enormous psychological as well as aesthetic benefits.

6   Colours

The colours around you, especially those of large flat surfaces such as walls, floors and filing cabinets, can have a profound effect on your moods and attitudes. If you are surrounded by grey or beige walls, dark brown or grey flooring, grey filing cabinets, and so on, it will not be easy for you to be creative, energetic and efficient. In this case, you must bring more life into the office with fresh flowers, colourful pictures and office stationery. If you can repaint your office, do not be afraid of colour since this can have a very energising effect. You should take the following precautions, however:

- It is usually better to have light, bright colours than either very strong or very weak colours
- They should have a 'freshness' or glow to them rather than appear flat or drab
- Avoid colour pollution – that is, having too many large swathes of different and contrasting colours in the same area

Specific colours have attributes that can be used to balance extreme office environments or to enhance any desired atmosphere. The following examples demonstrate this idea (*):

- Where noise and frantic activity characterise the working mode, the use of soft greens and blues will calm nerves and lower voices
- Where energetic creativity and brainstorming are needed to get the work done, yellow is most effective
- For work that requires deep thinking and imagination, soft blue or purple is helpful
- Routine tasks that require extended periods of concentration are supported by green
- To compensate for slow, uninspiring work, paint the walls in warm, soft yellow, orange or peach
- Rich creams or peach can be used for warm and inviting reception areas

7   Configuration

It is surprising how much subliminal stress can be created just from the way we arrange ourselves in an office. Some of the situations that can initiate such feelings of vulnerability and stress are:

* sitting for long periods with your back to a door, a very large window, a large open area or a corridor
* sitting directly in front of a door or very large window
* sitting for long periods in a large open area without 'protection' from the side or clear 'territorial' boundaries
* insufficient personal 'territory' to comfortably hold the work for which you are directly responsible
* facing a wall which is closer than about two metres
* directly facing someone else who is within about two metres from you
* having sharp corners and edges of walls or large items of furniture pointing directly at you
* working directly under large beams, overhead shelves or cupboards
* working in an office where you cannot see the whole space from each position (e.g. as an L-shaped office)

If possible, arrange your seating position to avoid the majority of these situations. If you have no choice but to sit with your back exposed to doors, corridors etc., make sure that you have a high-backed chair and that there is some object on your desk that can reflect what is going on behind you (e.g. a small mirror or shiny metal object). If you are forced to face a wall, put a broad landscape picture on it to give your primeval brain the idea that there is open space in front of you. Similarly, if you cannot see into part of your office because the view is blocked by a wall, use a landscape picture to create the illusion of an unobstructed view. Try to conceal, or distract attention from, sharp corners by strategically locating plants, lamps or other items.

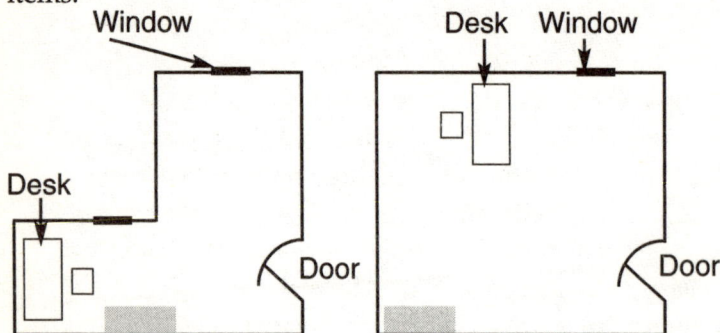

Bad desk position   Good desk position

Good and bad seating positions

Another related factor is the dimensions of the office or your 'territory' within the office. We humans feel most comfortable when the length, width and height of the room we are in conform to a certain classical ratio (1 to 1,618), sometimes called the *golden mean* (*). If your work area is long and narrow, you can symbolically expand it by putting broad landscape pictures on the sides, or adding more light to the sides while reducing the brightness at the ends. An excessively high ceiling can be made to appear lower by lowering light fittings or painting a thick line around the walls at a height. This tricks your subconscious mind into believing that the ceiling is lower than it actually is. If the ceiling is already too low, uplighters or images on the walls of upward-moving things (such as hot air balloons, flying birds, tall trees, towers etc) on the walls can compensate for this to some degree.

8   Air pollution

Modern office electronic equipment, furniture, wall and floor coverings, and air-conditioning systems are all sources of toxic chemicals. Your mind may not always be consciously aware of their presence, but your body responds to them anyway, and will be using some of your energy to fight off bacteria, toxins, free-radical molecules (primary cancer-causing agents) and dust particles. It is rarely possible these days to work without the aid of these materials and equipment, so we must take steps to reduce their effect. Here are some suggestions:

- Keep lots of plants that absorb common toxins (either through their roots or leaves) emitted from plastics, adhesives and solvents, such as formaldehyde, acetone, alcohol and toluene. Here is a list of examples taken from the book *Eco Friendly House Plants* by B. C. Wolverton. The plants selected are aesthetically pleasing from a feng shui point of view and are also very effective and easy to maintain (*): Boston fern, areca palm, bamboo palm, rubber plant, English ivy, ficus, peace lily, dumb cane, schefflera, king of hearts, dwarf banana, lily turf, spider plant, dwarf azalea, tulip.
- If possible, keep printers and photocopiers (a major source of pollutants and noise) in a separate ventilated room, or at least close to an openable window. There is a tendency for office cleaning staff to use an array of commercial cleaning materials for wiping down office furniture and equipment. These products, although they

may smell nice (well, sort of!), contain many toxic chemicals. It is better to use either eco-friendly products (available from most health-food shops or organic mail-order companies) or home-made solutions using vinegar, borax, baking soda, salt and lemon juice.

• Reduce dust levels by minimising open shelving and keeping flat surfaces free of books, files, papers and other clutter so that they can be wiped clean easily.

• Office cleaning is best done in the evenings, so that dust, stirred up by brushes or vacuum cleaners, has time to settle before you start to work there.

9   Electromagnetic radiation

All the cells of our bodies are little electrical devices with their own electromagnetic fields (EMFs). We evolved these systems over millions of years in the fairly stable electromagnetic environment of the earth. In the last 50

years or so, there has been a dramatic alteration of the
electromagnetic environment in which we live as a result of
all the electrical and electronic devices we use. Since all
EMFs interact with each other, our bodies are adversely
affected by this new environment at the atomic and
molecular levels. Studies in Europe and the USA link long-
term exposure to EMFs with a wide range of disorders
including depression, anxiety, hormonal imbalance,
immune-system breakdown, an inability to utilise nutrients
from food and the development of cancer cells.

There are four main approaches to this challenge:

1 Move as far away as possible from the sources of EMFs.
2 Minimise the use of high-EMF-emitting devices such as
   fluorescent light tubes, photocopying machines, laser
   printers, computers and mobile phones – i.e. turn them
   off as often as possible.
3 Suppress EMFs at source as much as possible by using
   electrical shielding, cork tiles under computers, printers
   etc. and bioprotection antennae which destructively
   interfere with the EMFs from computer screens. Certain
   plants are also supposed to absorb strong EMFs and
   release negatively charged oxygen atoms to compensate
   for the depletion of such atoms by the EMFs (which often
   makes offices seem 'stuffy' despite air conditioning).
   Ferns, evergreens and torch cactuses are recommended
   for this purpose (*).
4 Personal protection can be implemented in two main
   ways. First, there are a number of bioenergy resonators
   and balancing devices on the market. Some seem to
   work better than others, but it may depend on the
   individual. I have personally experienced changes in my

body energies with one of these devices that I carry in my shirt pocket. The effect was clearly measurable using medical diagnostic equipment (*). The second approach is to strengthen your biological systems through eating only organic food, using macrobiotic cookoing methods (the feng shui diet), taking appropriate exercise, drinking only properly filtered and energised water, and taking the right balance of nutritional supplemnts to provide the minerals, vitamins and antioxidants that 99 percent of us need to maintain dynamic health(*).

10   Geopathic stress

The Earth's magnetic field is fairly stable over time scales of thousands of years. Our biological systems have evolved in this field and do not work so well without it. There exist, however, very localised disturbances to this magnetic field that, for people who spend many hours each day in them, seem to cause a lowering of the human energy field, lethargy, depression and serious illnesses such as cancer. This phenomenon is called *geopathic stress*. It appears to be related to geologic faults in the earth's crust, or fast flowing underground streams of trapped water, or major underground earthworks such as foundations for high-rise buildings, main sewers and railways. It is worth mentioning that full scientific investigations of these phenomena still needs to be conducted, but the effects are well known and have been detected by dowsers for hundreds of years.

For most of human history, people have lived very close to nature and were probably more aware of sites which had odd magnetic forces around them (even though they had no idea of what it really was that felt odd), and chose to live or sleep elsewhere. The homes and businesses of modern urban society are situated for economic convenience rather than for environmental health, and our hurried, stress driven life styles leave no space for developing or experiencing the more subtle sensations and information that our bodies can give us. As a result, many people are working and sleeping on goepathic stress zones that can be a major contributor to all kinds of mental and physical illness.

So how would you know if your office is situated on a geopathic stress line? Let us first examine the clues.

1 Even if you look after plants correctly, do they still wither in this area?
2 Do you consistently suffer from inexplicable irritability in the office?
3 When in the office, do you keep getting strange illnesses or allergies that are reluctant to clear up?
4 Do you often feel tired and exhausted after only three or four hours at your desk?
5 Do you suffer from unexplained aches and pains?
6 Did the people who previously occupied your workspace have poor health or low performance?

If the answer to more than four or five of these questions is 'Yes', it is worth checking the office for geopathic stress. This is done by dowsing, which you can learn for yourself from books or courses, or you can hire an experienced person to do it for you (*).

If you suspect that geopathic stress is present in your office, the most important step is to move desks or chairs, where you sit for long periods each day, as far away as possible from the suspected geopathic stress line. If possible, move to a different part of the building and assign your current workspace as a storage area. In addition, there are a number of devices on the market that claim to reduce or eliminate geopathic stress by being plugged into the electrical ring main circuit (*). My experience with these devices has been mixed. Sometimes they seem to work, while in many situations they appear to have little or no effect. I have had more consistent results with the placement of mineral crystals such as salt, quartz, amethyst etc. on or near the geopathic stress lines. It seems that particular minerals affect only certain forms of geopathic stress, so it is necessary to dowse for the cure as well as for the presence of this phenomenon (*). Another common solution is to drive metal rods or tubes into the soil along the geopathic stress lines. This is not so easy, though, if your office is on the 23rd floor of a building in the middle of a concrete city centre.

An alternative and more cost-effective solution to counteracting geopathic stress effects can be provided by special versions of the bioenergy resonators described in the previous section. These small, passive devices apparently retune the unnatural energy field to one that is in harmony with those of human beings, animals and plants (*).

If you, or any of your colleagues are experiencing inexplicable emotional, mental or physical health problems at work, it is worthwhile checking for geopathic stress. At least purchase a passive bioenergy resonator, just to be on the safe side. It could save your career or your business!

Summary

In most offices that I have worked with, 'Wednesday', where we have been taking all the practical measures necessary to create a more supportive environment, is a very busy day for feng shui tasks. The pay-off, however, is very large and makes all the other feng shui adjustments for stimulating specific changes in your work life far more effective, and it is these that we will examine tomorrow.

Harmonising your workspace with your goals

Today, we look at using some additional feng shui techniques to customise the office environment for your own particular goals and objectives.

We can look at such customisation in terms of two main categories:

1 harmonising the office with your personal characteristics
2 harmonising the office with your personal goals and objectives

Harmonising the office with your personal characteristics

Your working environment must be compatible with your physical characteristics, otherwise you will waste much of your energy. The most common factors here are proper postural support from the chair(s) that you use (see the requirements described in Wednesday's tasks) and the lighting level. As you get older, you need more light by which to see clearly. Therefore, if you are over 40, you may genuinely need a desk lamp or other form of additional task lighting.

Another aspect of feng shui that we have not mentioned so far deals with the personality traits that are related to your birthdate. This is feng shui astrology. In the same way that our energy levels vary on a daily cycle, which in turn is

modulated by a monthly cycle and a yearly cycle, it has been observed that we also follow a nine-year cycle. It is well established in Western astrology that life patterns and certain character tendencies are related to the date and month of birth. In a similar way, feng shui astrology suggests that some key patterns or themes in your life correspond to the year in which you were born and at what stage of the cosmic 9-year cycle that year was. Thus, people born nine years apart are likely to have similar types of challenges or attributes in their lives. In addition to this, feng shui astrology can indicate how your particular set of challenges and attributes are modulated by the changing cosmic energies of each successive year. This is far too big a subject to cover fully in this book, so I recommend *Feng Shui Astrology* by Jon Sandifer as a good primer (*). We can, however, use the basics of this subject to help customise your working environment.

The first step is to find out the type of year you were born in. Each year in the cycle is referred to by a number from 1 to 9. The chart below defines the year numbers of recent

decades. One important point to remember is that the
Chinese year usually begins within the first two weeks of
February in the Gregorian calendar. So if you were born on
say 1 February 1968, your birth year is 1967 in feng shui
astrology terms.

9	8	7	6	5	4	3	2	1
1928	1929	1930	1931	1932	1933	1934	1935	1936
1937	1938	1939	1940	1941	1942	1943	1944	1945
1946	1947	1948	1949	1950	1951	1952	1953	1954
1955	1956	1957	1958	1959	1960	1961	1962	1963
1964	1965	1966	1967	1968	1969	1970	1971	1972
1973	1974	1975	1976	1977	1978	1979	1980	1981

Feng shui astrology year – type numbers

Some typical characteristics for each of these numbers are
briefly summarised as follows:-

1 Can be either lively and adventurous or sensitive and
   philosophical. Being quite confident and flexible, they are
   often good in negotiations or arbitration situations, but do
   need some clear channel in which to focus their energy.
   Under stress they can be very anxious and shy.
2 Steady, reliable and helpful are the main attributes, and
   they can be good organisers or teachers. They can show
   diplomacy and tact, but the negative side of this
   character is cynical and suspicious with a tendency to
   leave jobs unfinished.
3 Focus tends to be on 'doing' rather than 'being', and thus
   will often appear spontaneous and active. Usually

positive and optimistic, setting new ideas and grandiose plans in motion – but prefer to leave the details for others to sort out. Can be opinionated and direct yet witty in their communications, which may lead them into trouble.

4 Emotions can fluctuate quickly from calm and easy-going to being stubborn and impulsive. They are very trusting (often too trusting) and, while being innovative and creative, are also practical, with sensitivity to all aspects of a situation. Can be very charismatic leaders.

5 Must be at the centre of what ever is happening, and like to take control. This can lead to over-involvement and a life of extreme 'ups and downs'. Very good in times of change however, being determined and resilient to setbacks.

6 As natural leaders and authorities, are often the 'ground-breakers' in society. Tend to hold to strong ethical values while being rational, ordered and careful to the point of rigidity at times. Perfectionism and self criticism are also common traits, but they do not like being criticised by others.

7 Good at entertaining and relating to others, which tends to place them in leadership positions where guidance and direction are key factors. They prefer independence and freedom to long-term commitments. Can be charismatic speakers yet have a deep, reflective, spiritual side. Get depressed and withdrawn when frustrated.

8 Single minded approach to business generally, tending to learn from experience, moving carefully and consistently, rather than with great subtlety or creativity. They have enormous reserves of energy and hidden strength, yet often appear reserved and uncommunicative. Great sense of fairness and justice.

9 Energetic and inspiring, able to handle fluctuating situations well and initiate change where necessary. Can often find a path through difficult situations and are very attentive to details. Although projecting a confident image, deeper sensitivities can erupt stormily at times.

The second step is to find out the 'physical archetypal energy' that your particular year number represents. In feng shui there are five of these archetypes, which are given the names, 'earth', 'metal', 'water', 'wood' and 'fire', and are often referred to as 'the five elements'. Each of these has a range of physical characteristics associated with it, as shown below:

Year numbers	9	2, 5, 8	6, 7	1	3, 4
Energy name	FIRE	EARTH	METAL	WATER	WOOD
Shape	pointed	flat	dome	wavy	tall & slim
Movement	expand/ contract	converge	condense	flowing	up & out
Colours	red/purple	yellow/ brown	white/ grey	blue/ black	green
Material	fire	stone, sand, earth, ceramic	metal, hard plastic	water, glass	wood, plants

The concept here is that the physical phenomena are metaphors for the normal temperament of someone born in a particular year. You have probably already heard of people described as 'having a firey temperament', 'down to earth', 'hard as nails (metal)', 'rock solid', 'weak (i.e. not firm or fixed) as water' etc. These simple statements are an attempt to give you a 'taste' of a complex personality characteristic in a similar (although less refined) way to the five-element model.

Before we can discuss how to use this information for customising your workplace, it is necessary to reveal another classic feng shui model. This places these five natural energy archetypes or 'elements' in relationship to each other, as shown in the diagram.

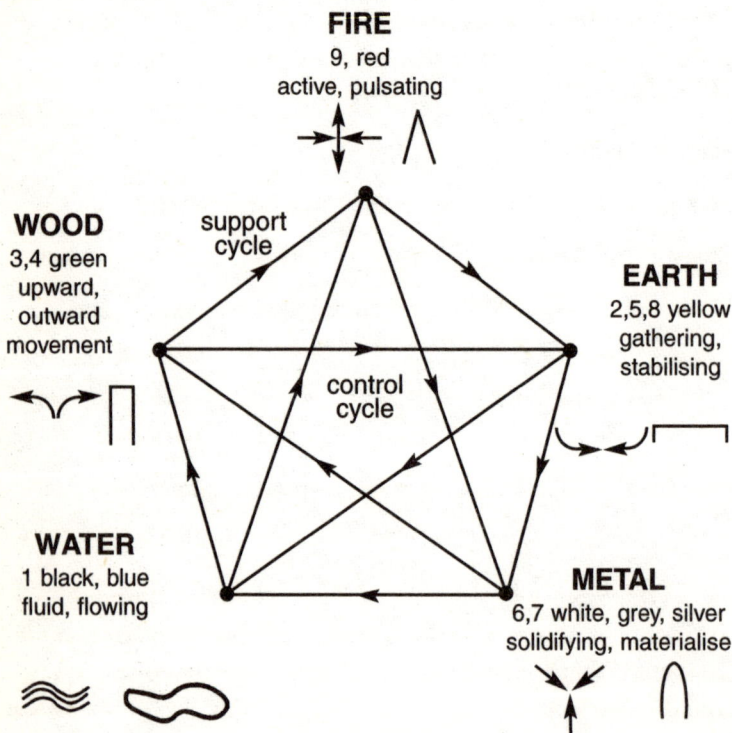

FIRE
9, red
active, pulsating

WOOD
3,4 green
upward,
outward
movement

support
cycle

EARTH
2,5,8 yellow
gathering,
stabilising

control
cycle

WATER
1 black, blue
fluid, flowing

METAL
6,7 white, grey, silver
solidifying, materialise

The five-element model

Two kinds of relationship are shown here: supportive and controlling. In the supportive relationships, the characteristics of one element are enhanced or supported by the characteristics of the preceding one. Thus 'Earth'-type energies are reinforced by 'Fire'-type energies. So, if you were born in 1971, your primary feng shui astrology number is '2', and you will tend to feel quite at home in 'earth'-type environments. When feeling vulnerable, however, having some 'fire' around (red things, for example) will tend to make you feel more supported. Interestingly, the following element in this cycle ('metal' in our current example) is a metaphor for the major challenges in your life, or the characteristics that will enhance your personal growth the most.

Let me give you a personal example. I am a 'metal' person, and I like my surroundings to be ordered, I keep data in a well-structured filing system and rely heavily on plans and 'to-do' lists. My biggest challenge in this life is to develop 'water' characteristics, that is to feel comfortable being spontaneous, adapting to unexpected situations and delving deep in contemplation. To help me maintain progress in this way I have a blue curvy logo for my business, and keep an array of blue clothes. I also have pictures of water on the wall of my office.

In the 'control' type of relationships, the characteristics of one element are influenced by those opposite them. This influence is subtly different from the 'support' type of relationship. Here, a little 'fire' can have a stimulating effect on a 'metal', person, but excessive 'fire' dominates and oppresses 'metal', which can lead to irritation, a lack of focus or insufficient attention to the details. Being a 'metal type' person, if I worked in an office, therefore, with a 9, fire-type colleague, I may be inspired by that person at times. But if that person was being very '9-type' for hours on end, I would tend to feel very irritated. To deal with an excess of 'fire' energy around me, therefore, I could soften the effect with 'earth'-type colours and materials, or suppress it with blues, blacks and watery images.

Personality clashes are not unusual in large office situations. If you study feng shui astrology, you can see how such clashes can arise as people's dominant behaviours shift from month to month and from year to year between various degrees of harmony and discord. Becoming aware of these fluctuations and how they interact can make you less affected by them. Of course, if you feel constantly irritated or intimidated by someone in the office, you can symbolically disperse such apparent 'negative energy' by discretely placing a small, convex mirror (or some other object with a reflecting convex surface) on your desk between you and them. You will find that this individual will then become less intrusive. You can use the same trick for other irritations too: the source of a persistent noise, the sharp corner of a wall or item of furniture 'pointing' at you etc.

Another factor associated with your primary feng shui astrological number is a compass direction as follows:

1 = north; 2 = south-west; 3 = east; 4 = south-east; 5 = centre; 6 = north-west; 7 = west; 8 = north-east; 9 = south.

According to some texts, the direction corresponding to your astrological number is said to be the best way for you to sit for maximum results or for locating particular types of activity. In my experience, however, there are far more influential factors on performance than these, such as the layout of the office, lighting, noise, colours, etc. Anyway, most of us have little control over which way round we sit in the typical busy, overcrowded office.

Harmonising the office with your personal goals and objectives

It is important that our surroundings not only support what we are doing but also actually symbolise or represent what we want to achieve or the experience of working life that we want to have. There are two parts to this. First, establish features in the office to create an atmosphere which is, in a very general way, supporting any business-oriented goals that you have. Second, install specific and carefully placed objects that directly symbolise the concrete results you want.

For the general 'tuning' process you can use the 'Five-element model' described above to help set the right tone. The list below describes the style of environment that is representative of each primary 'element':

- FIRE: very energetic and lively. These are great environments for stimulating activity, but they can also be exhausting, and they are not appropriate for concentration or deep thought.
- EARTH: these are places where people tend to gather, and where fundamentals of problems or activities can be seen more clearly. They stimulate discussion and give a sense of support, but in excess they can feel restrictive and obstructive.
- METAL: these are rather cold and rigid, but they can be good for getting down to work and focussing on specific things for sharp, quick results. They can be striking to look at, but they tend not to be particularly relaxing.
- WATER: these are cool and flexible. Ideas can flow easily here, and deep emotions can be explored. They are not appropriate, however, where stability is a key issue.
- WOOD: these are places for starting new projects and generating new ways of doing things. They are quite calming, and therefore good where concentration is required.

In feng shui, the environment is said to be 'balanced' when the characteristics of each of these 'elements' are present in one form or another, in proportions that support the intended function of the space. Simply use your imagination to create the balance you need in any particular room and let your subconscious mind do the rest for you.

Thus, if you need to enhance, say, 'earth' in your environment (for example, you may feel the need for more nurturing or stability in your work), then add more 'earth'-related colours, materials and shapes around you. Also, add a little 'fire' to your desk in the form of, say, red pens, a mouse mat, files, stapler, etc. But don't overdo it: if 'fire' is too strong and does not respect the characteristics of 'earth', it has the opposite effect and you will feel smothered and entrapped. You can use these relationships in reverse as well. So if there is too much 'fire' in your life (say you are hyperactive, surrounded by noise and have lots of brightly coloured things around you, and your boss is a 9-type person), you can reduce the stress of all this by increasing the 'earth' characteristics of your space. 'Earth' feeds off or drains 'fire' energies. Alternatively, you can suppress the effects by adding 'water' characteristics (i.e. real water or blues and blacks) to your surroundings. This can, however, create a sense of great tension if done to excess. This is acceptable if you want to make a quick, clear and decisive change in your career or business, but it will be difficult to tolerate, and be quite exhausting over extended periods.

Another approach to general harmonising is to use colours, positive images, plants etc. that are associated with the business or work that you do. Here is an example of this idea. A distributor of Italian kitchenware was not achieving sales targets. Amongst various structural and organisational problems, the sales office was poorly lit and had very drab colours on the walls and floor. In addition, there were no images of either the kitchenware or of Italy to stimulate and inspire the sales staff. Instead, the walls were either bare, or cluttered with totally irrelevant, or uninspiring pictures. To liven up the atmosphere of this office, part of the solution was to replace the irrelevant pictures on the walls with classic Italian scenes and with images of the kitchenware they were selling. We also suggested improving the quality of lighting and colours of the walls and floor to give a more Italian 'feel' to the environment.

To symbolise and stimulate the specific results that you want, you need to place carefully selected objects in certain critical positions in your workspace. Here is how to do it.

On Monday you defined your main goals and objectives, and related some of them to the nine key aspects of life. You also saw that you need to work on the complementary aspect as well as the one that is primarily associated with your goal. Each aspect of life was associated with a specific number from 1 to 9, and arranged in a very specific pattern. There is some significance in this pattern that we do not need to elaborate on here. The important point however, is that you can use this pattern to assign each aspect of life to an area in your office, work area or desktop.

There are two basic models for doing this. One model assigns aspects of life to locations according to the compass directions. If you look back to the early part of this chapter, you will see that the same numbers that are associated with the aspects of life are also linked to years, personality types and compass directions. This model (and its variants from different parts of Asia) tends to be rather cumbersome for assigning aspects of life to spaces especially in modern working and living environments. Another model, which tends to be more practical, assigns the aspects of life pattern to spaces according to where you enter or approach your office work area or desk. This is the method we shall use here.

Draw a map of your office or desk space and mark the
'nine aspects of life' over it, with the entrance (or direction
in which you approach it) in one of the segments named
either 'Self awareness' (⑧), 'Path/career' (①) or 'Helpers,
friends, experience' (⑥). This is shown in the diagrams.

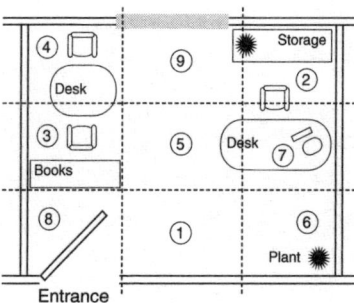

Segmented office space   *Segmented desk space*

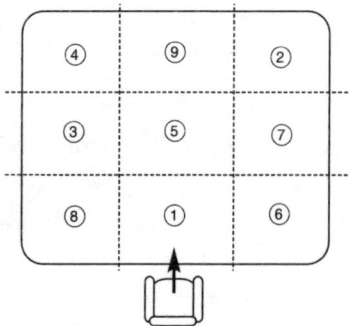

The next step is to select what you want to represent your
goal or intention with. Here are some possibilities.

For emphasising or boosting the energy in a particular aspect of office life, various 'tools' can be used, including:

- moving objects (fish, clocks with pendulum or second hand etc.)
- extra lights
- refracting glass balls (if direct sunlight is available)
- brightly coloured or shiny objects, decorative pieces and pictures
- vigorous, bright plants
- wind chimes (if exposed to a draft, the sound of these can be irritating to people around you)
- mirrors (use with great caution in a work environment. They must be carefully placed to avoid reflecting yourself at work, any untidiness or chaos, other people, unpleasant sights from outside such as heavy traffic, delapidated buildings etc.)
- mobiles, 'executive toys'
- models or images of what you want to have happen

Select energising objects which are of a style or design which matches the general office décor or style of work.

I once visited the very elegantly designed office of a high class PR agency. The manager placed a 'ba-gua' mirror (a little round mirror set in an eight-sided plywood frame, painted red and green with the classical trigrams marked on each of the sides) on one of the toilet doors to 'protect the office from negative energy'. This cheaply made and cheap looking thing looked so out-of-place that it actually drew attention to the toilet rather than have the opposite effect — which was what was actually intended.

In another office, the owner of the company was persuaded that she could 'energise' the sales staff by putting a rocking and rotating 'executive toy' on their desks. This device was constructed of poor quality black plastic and chrome plated wire, and made an annoying click every second as it moved. The sales staff were not impressed, and sales did not increase!

Success in a job is often strongly dependent upon cooperation, mutual support and affection in a group or team. To encourage harmony in such a situation, if this is needed, you can energise the 'Relationships, marriage' area of your office or desk space, using any of the methods described above. Alternatively, you can place an image or other physical representation of an harmonious team or group of the same number (comprising people, animals or even inanimate objects) in the appropriate area. You then should energise your 'Self-awareness' area to symbolise learning more about yourself and what drives your feelings and behaviours under pressure. Don't forget to actually investigate yourself, through books, seminars, counsellors etc. Again, your own intuition and imagination can be brought to bear in selecting ways to remind your subconcious about what it needs to work on, while the rest of you handles regular daily tasks.

Perhaps you consider that it is time that you were promoted in your job, but opportunities are not presenting themselves to you. In this case, you could energise the 'career' area of, say, your desk space. You could put a piece of bright red carpet under your feet. If people ask you what it is for, you can always say that it provides extra comfort for your feet, if those people are not turned into the concepts of feng shui. Alternatively, stick some red tape to the front edge of the desk, or under the computer keyboard if it normally sits in the 'career' area of your desk. At the opposite edge of the desk, in the 'recognition' area, place bright or shiny objects, or something that specifically symbolises the position that you want. You might also put a little message to yourself there, in some sort of code if you prefer, saying 'I have the job!'. Just making the effort to represent in physical form the outcome that you want, is enough to set your subconscious mind working on ways to achieve it. All you need to do is follow-up on the ideas it comes up with — which can appear while you are waiting for the bus, in the check-out queue, planning tomorrow's dinner or even in your dreams.

While you may tend to focus on what you would like to change or improve in your work situation, there will probably be some aspects that are working well for you already. Your objective then might be to stabilise the situation. In this case, the symbolic tools that you might consider include:-

- heavy stones or rocks
- heavy or large furniture
- solid statues, stone pots
- paper weights
- picture of something solid (mountain, rock, elephant, etc.)

Consider an example of using feng shui to ensure that a positive situation is maintained. Let us say that you receive very good support and advice from your boss or other more experienced persons in the company. However, you hear that this person may be intending to leave for one reason or another, an you would like to ensure that the help he or she gave you continues in some form. To symbolically stabilise the benefits you are receiving, place something appropriate that represents to you the idea of solidity or immovability in the 'Parents/Teachers/Past' area of your

office or desk. Such action will lock into your subconscious mind the idea of stabilizing the situation, so that you will automatically act in such a way that you will continue to receive, in some form, advice from this person. You do, however, need to be open as to how this advice may come. Any number of possibilities could happen with this individual, such as:

1 They will not leave, and will continue to advise you as before.
2 They will leave, yet keep in touch with you anyway because of the relationship you have now.
3 They will leave but offer you all their books or papers, which will enable you to manage perfectly well without their physical presence.

4 They will leave eventually but be willing to educate or
   train you as necessary in the meantime, so that you can
   carry on without them.

The manifestation of events is not critical. The important
point is that you are using your workspace to remind your
subconscious of your intention to continue drawing on
someone's particular knowledge and experience from the
past. This means that you may also need to be creative in
maintaining the links you have with your advisor or in
developing the knowledge or skills you need to act as your
advisor. So energise the corresponding 'Creativity, children'
area of your office or desk, by any of the options given
earlier.

Getting 'the best bang for the buck'

At this stage, you may have quite a long list of actions necessary to unblock your environment, liberate more of your vitality and creativity, and tune your workplace to harmonise with your new purpose, vision, mission or specific goals and objectives. The next big question is: 'What will give me the best and fastest return for my investment of time and money?'

The first step is to divide the actions into those required for creating a generally low-stress and supportive office space (or desk space if that is all that you have) and those that are for stimulating a specific outcome. It is important to do as much stress reduction as possible before stimulating specific outcomes.

Consider first the actions for general stress and energy-drain reductions. Place each action in a subcategory such as:

- reducing physical stress and strain (e.g. an unsupportive chair, poor lighting, polluted air, potential electromagnetic or geopathic stress)
- reducing obstructions to physical movement (e.g. a seating position that is too cramped, awkward access to file cabinets, an overcrowded office)
- reducing psychological stress and strain (e.g. sitting with your back to a window or door, drab or inappropriate colour schemes, broken or damaged things around you)
- reducing obstructions to clear thinking (e.g. excessive noise, being surrounded by clutter, unfinished work)

Within these subcategories you can prioritise the different actions by determining what negative features seem to recur, which create the greatest imbalance or contrast and which are the most extreme. To explain what I mean by these factors, here are some examples.

Recurring themes:

- Clutter everywhere – in the entrance, on the noticeboard, in the kitchen area, around your desk, on your desk, in the desk drawers, on the computer start-up screen, in your personal organiser, briefcase, handbag, etc. People working in this kind of environment would tend to feel overwhelmed, scattered and exhausted.
- Drabness – grey walls, floor, furniture, filing cabinets, pictures and so on, coupled with poor-quality lighting. This creates an atmosphere of 'stuckness' and lethargy with nothing happening.

- Shabbiness – dirty or flaking paintwork, scratched, chipped or broken furniture, lighting that does not work, old and worn-out computer equipment stuffed into corners or behind squeaking doors. On the desks you may find jammed-up staplers, dried-out pens, broken pencils and broken drawer handles. This theme fosters mistakes, low standards of work and lots of incompletions.

Harsh contrasts:

The second key element to look for is strong or harsh contrasts in the environment. An example of this was in the office of a firm of architects. In one area, three of the walls were covered in large panels painted red, black and white. The fourth wall was all glass. Nobody could work comfortably in this space. Another common form of discomforting contrast occurs in wide open-plan offices with large windows along one side and inadequate lighting on the opposite side.

Excesses:

Finally, pick out what there may be too much of. For example, if all of the walls are bright yellow, the energy can be overwhelming after a couple of hours. Perhaps there is just too much furniture, too many pictures or too much noise.

You now have the basis of a good plan for reducing the main environmental stresses and energy drains. However, an assessment of costs and time investment is necessary before you can initiate it. There is usually a trade-off here between the potential benefits (which are sometimes not immediately calculable) and what can be afforded, what is most urgent or what will give minimum disruption to ongoing work.

I recommend a 'two pronged' approach. If there would be a clear and substantial benefit from some change that requires a significant investment on the part of the business, immediately start the process of enrolling your colleagues in the project and initiating the approval and funding process. In the meantime, start doing the important actions that cost very little or no money – such as clearing the clutter, changing the pictures and images around you, or putting some plants on your desk. Usually, most of the actions and many of the benefits are in this low-cost category. It is important also to be persistent. If your workplace is very unsupportive, it may seem almost impossible to change the atmosphere within your lifetime. But you would be surprised at how every little step energises you for the next one: gradually everything changes, and you can begin to implement the actions for stimulating your specific goals and objectives.

IT CAN BE DONE ... IT CAN BE DONE

Warning! If your office is in a really big mess or is too
energy draining because of some or all of the factors
described on Wednesday, do not stimulate the aspects
associated with your goals and objectives. First, you may
inadvertently create more chaos, and second, you may not
have the energy to take any opportunities that might
emerge.

Finally, there may come a time when even persistent action
is not enough to transform your office environment.
Perhaps the changes needed are so interlocked that it is
impossible to implement them efficiently. Or perhaps the
work is piling up so fast that there is no time at all to make
the office function better. In such a case, nothing short of a
revolution is necessary: a complete gutting, redesign and
rebuilding of the space to suit the current workload. Such
drastic action requires a great deal of reflection on what
you really need and how best to make it happen. Then you
must plan carefully, taking as much feng shui advice as you
need to ensure the optimum result is obtained.

Now at last we can start those actions that can harmonise the office or workspace with the specific results you want, as defined on Monday. I suggest the following approach:

- Start with one small goal. This can be a small component of a much larger goal that has a high priority for you.
- Initially make small, discrete, low-cost energising or stabilising adjustments as necessary. Starting with dramatic or flamboyant changes can indicate a superficial attitude and result in a negative reaction.
- Notice what happens, and make further adjustments if required.
- When satisfied with the results, work on other small goals until you gain confidence in the process.
- Gradually make larger changes to support more important goals, as circumstances allow.

Being a person whose feng shui astrology numbers are very 'metal' biased, I prefer to define any process or system in a fairly structured way. So, I have constructed the following flow diagram to help you (or at least fellow 6's, 7's and possibly a few 4's as well) to visualise a logical, practical and cost-effective way of approaching your office feng shui project. Tomorrow we will examine the process of keeping this flow going.

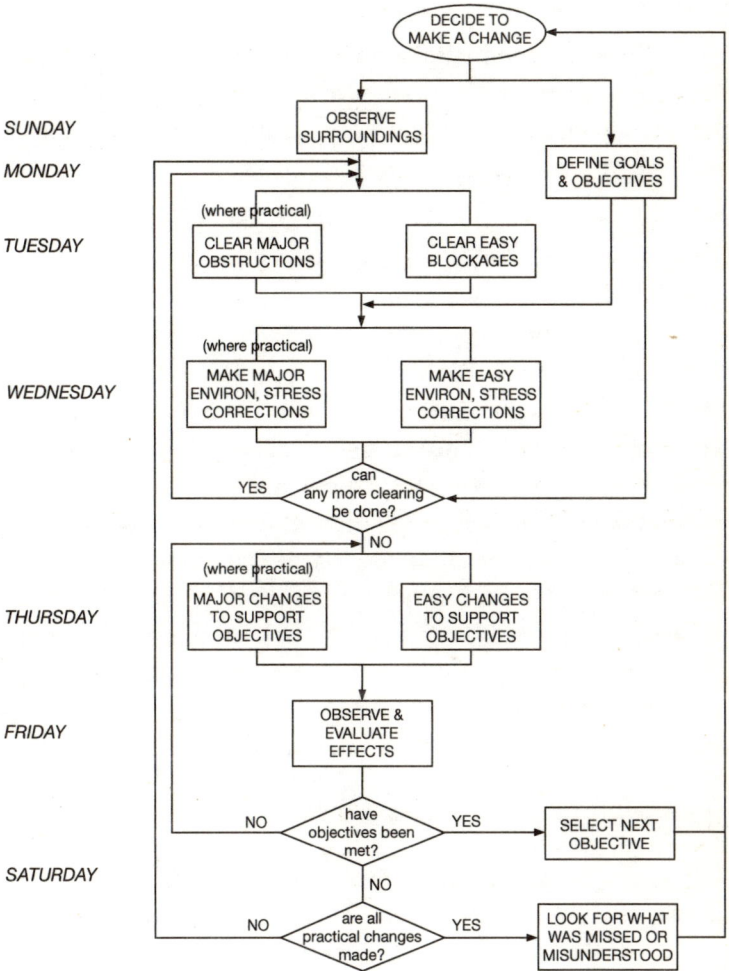

	DECIDE TO MAKE A CHANGE
SUNDAY	OBSERVE SURROUNDINGS
MONDAY	DEFINE GOALS & OBJECTIVES
TUESDAY	(where practical) CLEAR MAJOR OBSTRUCTIONS — CLEAR EASY BLOCKAGES
WEDNESDAY	(where practical) MAKE MAJOR ENVIRON, STRESS CORRECTIONS — MAKE EASY ENVIRON, STRESS CORRECTIONS
	can any more clearing be done? — YES / NO
THURSDAY	(where practical) MAJOR CHANGES TO SUPPORT OBJECTIVES — EASY CHANGES TO SUPPORT OBJECTIVES
FRIDAY	OBSERVE & EVALUATE EFFECTS
	have objectives been met? — NO / YES — SELECT NEXT OBJECTIVE
SATURDAY	are all practical changes made? — NO / YES — LOOK FOR WHAT WAS MISSED OR MISUNDERSTOOD

Simplified feng shui action flow diagram

Keeping your workspace working for you

Now that you have made some changes to your workplace or office you will notice that there is a new – hopefully more comfortable and inspiring – 'feel' or sense of vitality about it. You have altered the *chi* of the space.

Our overall experience of a space is a combination of our interpretation of all that our senses pick up: light, heat, sound, temperature, smell, texture, shapes etc. This combination of various forms or energy is called *chi* (pronounced 'chee'). We, as individuals, also have a personal chi that includes factors such as vitality, temperament, appearance and so on. There is also a chi of a group of people working together or within the same office environment. Since we are all different, the effect on our personal chi from the chi of any particular environment will also be different. However, your office environment, or particular features of it, can be said to have good chi or bad chi depending on how it normally affects you. Another factor that influences our experience of a space is how it directs our attention. This is sometimes called the 'flow of chi'. A comfortable room does not have too many large distractions or openings to the outside world.

Although you may not have heard it expressed in this way before, you are already well aware of these phenomena. You know that some places feel better than others although you may not always be able to pin-point exactly what it is that is creating the difference. Feng shui helps to identify these factors so that you can do something about them.

Of course there is no absolute quantification of chi. Our
actual experience of a space will depend on our own
varying chi and on environmental variables such as light,
weather, season, temperature etc. The act of altering the chi
of your working environment with a specific intention in
mind will also create ripples of change that can spread to
many aspects of your career and life in general.

You now need to decide what is next on your list of
objectives or improvements and adjust the chi of your
space accordingly. Feng shui is a continuing process, not a
'one-off' job. It is important therefore, once a week, to
review the effects of any changes you have made. Look for
effects along the lines that you had intended, and also note
what else might have happened (side-effects perhaps).

If your feng shui actions have worked and what you
desired has occurred, then it is appropriate to decide on
your next goal and what corresponding feng shui will
support you in that. Alternatively, if you feel the need to

solidify a new situation, bring in some earth element (such as a rock or something earth coloured) to a position that represents the change you have achieved. In the example described on Thursday, for stimulating a promotion at work, it was suggested to place a red rug under your chair or a piece of red tape on the front edge of your desk (the 'Career/path' area). Also, something bright and energetic was to be placed at the opposite edge of your desk (the 'Recognition' area). Now you have been given a promotion, but you are on probation for a couple of months to see how you get on in the new position. At this point you could exchange the energising features on your desk for solidifying or grounding ones. Just making these actions will create a subconscious anchor in your mind that will then figure out by itself what to do to solidify your achievement.

The feng shui solutions that you made for a particular, time-limited objective should be removed once the objective has been obtained, otherwise the messages being sent to your mind are irrelevant and this can reduce the potential effect of future feng shui actions.

What if the feng shui changes you made seem to have brought about very different results from those you intended? Say, for example, instead of getting the promotion you wanted, you were moved to a completely different job or were fired. This should prompt you to ask some very deep and interesting questions, such as:

• 'Was I certain that promotion in my current line of work was what I really wanted?' The benefits may have been obvious, but did you really consider the downsides also:

perhaps being stuck in a business that was not developing, being 'typecast' in a particular role, thus blocking further promotion opportunities, feeling ready to take on more responsibility and accountability and yet knowing deep down that this job would not really offer enough challenge?

- 'Were my actions purely for getting the promotion because I wanted to be of greater service, or was there an element of aggression in them?' Was it a case of: 'I'll block so-and-so from getting promotion if I possibly can'; 'I'll get the job so that I can take revenge or have power over someone'; or 'The guys at the club will be impressed with my new title'? When you use feng shui in earnest, it is quite powerful – as are the consequences if you misuse it.

Perhaps, instead of getting a promotion in the office in Manchester, you found yourself being offered the chance to work for a year or two in Hawaii and were given a large financial compensation package. This could be the best and easiest (and most idyllic) way for you to develop your career and be acknowledged for what you do.

Perhaps, instead of getting a promotion, you found yourself getting married. Well, you activated your 'Career/path' and 'Recognition' areas, and maybe your relationship is currently far more important to you than the job. So you got a proposal to move to the next level in that relationship.

What if nothing seemed to have happened after your feng shui changes? In this case, you need to ask yourself whether the changes you made were appropriate and whether you really wanted the outcome they were designed for. Also think about how sincere you were in implementing them. Half-hearted efforts are unlikely to bring results because you do not create a sufficiently strong 'anchor' for your mind to latch onto, so it fails to respond.

I have a wonderful client near Munich whose company was on the verge of bankruptcy because he could not find major investors to support the manufacture and marketing of a new technology they had developed. He was very despondent and very sceptical about feng shui, but in desperation (and under dire threats from his secretary if he didn't) he decided to have a consultation. We talked long and hard about applying the principles on his office design (which was grey all over with a few dull, desolate landscape pictures and black furniture), the company logo and corporate image, personnel issues, and development strategy. Then, despite his scepticism, he went ahead with typical German rigour and determination, and started to implement our suggestions. He moved his desk to a more protected position, added energy (in the form of a fish tank) to the 'prosperity' area, solidified an exposed corner in the 'relationships' area with a large plant container, removed the dull, uninspiring pictures and added a light to the 'creativity' area. He then followed up on the creative ideas we had discussed for financing his main business project. Several weeks later he called me. 'Herr Gunn', he said, 'I do not believe in this feng shui... but... somehow... I now have an endorsement from the German government and 2 million deutschemarks to complete our new product range.' Magic happens when you are sincere.

Remember that feng shui *is* a methodology for harnessing your surroundings to support the manifestation of your deepest desires. It is *not* a set of dogmatic rules for changing 'karma', or a magical cure for all known problems, or an alternative to doing something concrete about the challenges that office life provides.

So, learn more about the interaction between yourself and your environment from books, workshops or consultants, and experiment with the guidelines given to you. Also, however, use your commonsense and imagination, then keep track of the results from the changes that you make. In this way, you establish another tool for influencing the direction of your life towards the visions and image that you want to create for yourself.

If you run a business (or become someone who runs a business after following the advice in this book!), you can extend the principles of feng shui to harmonise the entire business facility, marketing materials, signs and logos with your corporate goals and image. There can hardly be a more cost-effective way of directing a company's success.

FENG SHUI FOR SUCCESS

BUSINESS   VISION   GOALS   ENVIRONMENT

Guide to resources

Further information on books, devices, organisations and services marked with the symbol (*) in the text, has been compiled in separate data sheets. These also give details of how or where to obtain the products and services described. The subjects covered include:-

General Office Environment Workshops and Consultations

- Feng shui principles and applications
- Project management
- Organising and structuring your business information

Feng Shui in Your External Office Environment

- Office furniture designs
- Light, lighting systems and health
- Colour and colour planning
- Testing for and dealing with geopathic stress
- Protecting yourself from excessive electromagnetic radiation
- Improving indoor air quality
- Beneficial and useful indoor plants

Feng Shui in Your Internal Body Environment

- Detoxifying your body to unleash vitality
- Non-toxic personal care systems
- Supplementing your diet for dynamic health
- Water and water quality – the key to well being
- Individual feng shui astrological information

The data sheets, and details of consulting services and workshops, can be obtained by writing to Integral Dynamics UK, PO Box 24422, London W5 4YG, United Kingdom, or by calling 0181 387 9266, or by e-mailing: gg@intedyn.co.uk

From the 'I Ching'

Hsiao Ch'u

小畜

An individual, when he has no authority or power to effect great changes directly in the outer world, can, none-the-less, influence events by refining the expression of his inner nature in small ways.

The 'I Ching' is a classic Chinese text of philosophic concepts that has been in its present form for about two thousand years, although its origins are much older. It provides the basis of feng shui in that it emphasises the relationship between managing one's life effectively and efficiently, and the examples of harmony and balance shown to us in nature.